GLOBAL EFFECTS

THE IMPACT OF SCIENCE, TECHNOLOGY, AND ECONOMICS IN SOUTHWEST ASIA AND NORTH AFRICA

CHRISTINE HONDERS

Published in 2021 by The Rosen Publishing Group, Inc.
29 East 21st Street, New York, NY 10010

First Edition

Editor: Siyavush Saidian
Book Design: Tanya Dellaccio

Photo Credits: Cover Bloomberg/Getty Images; p. 5 Nick Brundle Photography/Moment Open/Getty Images; p. 7 PeterHermesFurian/iStock.com; p. 9 David Steele/Shutterstock.com; p. 10 Dorling Kindersley/Getty Images; p. 11 https://upload.wikimedia.org/wikipedia/commons/thumb/e/e1/Xerxes_Cuneiform_Van.JPG/800px-Xerxes_Cuneiform_Van.JPG; p. 12 https://upload.wikimedia.org/wikipedia/commons/f/fd/Flake_Tool_MET_25.10.12i_EGDP011386.jpg; p. 13 arturbo/E+/Getty Images; p. 15 https://upload.wikimedia.org/wikipedia/commons/2/2d/Te_lawrence.jpg; p. 19 (left) General Photographic Agency/Hulton Archive/Getty Images; p. 19 (right) Hulton Deutsch/Corbis Historical/Getty Images; p. 21 ABDULLAH DOMA/AFP/Getty Images; p 23 winhorse/iStock/Getty Images Plus/Getty Images; p. 25 (top) IVAN KUZKIN/Shutterstock.com; p. 25 (bottom) Peter Hermes Furian/Shutterstock.com; p. 29 Starcevic/E+/Getty Images.

Cataloging-in-Publication Data

Names: Honders, Christine.
Title: The impact of science, technology, and economics in Southwest Asia and North Africa / Christine Honders.
Description: New York : PowerKids Press, 2021. | Series: Global effects | Includes glossary and index.
Identifiers: ISBN 9781725322400 (pbk.) | ISBN 9781725322424 (library bound) | ISBN 9781725322417 (6 pack) | ISBN 9781725322431 (ebook)
Subjects: LCSH: Middle East–Juvenile literature. | Middle East–Economic conditions–Juvenile literature. | Technology–Middle East. | Science–Middle East.
Classification: LCC DS44.H5866 2021 | DDC 956–dc23

Manufactured in the United States of America

CPSIA Compliance Information: Batch #CSPK20: For Further Information contact Rosen Publishing, New York, New York at 1-800-237-9932

CONTENTS

A GLOBAL RELATIONSHIP

Southwest Asia and North Africa is region rich in resources. Despite its status as a global superpower, the United States doesn't have enough natural resources to support its needs. It depends on the oil-rich nations in southwest Asia and North Africa for fuel. Fuel keeps homes warm, food cold, and store shelves filled.

The relationship between the wider world and the region of southwest Asia and North Africa is based on oil. Countries in this region went from being some of the world's poorest to some of the world's richest when oil reserves were discovered. Southwest Asia and North Africa instantly became major players in the world economy. Even before then, however, economics, science, and technology shaped and changed the region's relationship with the rest of the world.

FAST FACT

THE EARLY-20TH CENTURY DISCOVERY OF OIL IN SOUTHWEST ASIA AND NORTH AFRICA CHANGED LIFE IN THE REGION. EXISTING GOVERNMENTS BECAME FAR MORE POWERFUL AS THEY SOLD THE VALUABLE RESOURCE.

FOSSIL FUEL: MATTER FORMED OVER MILLIONS OF YEARS FROM PLANT AND ANIMAL REMAINS THAT IS BURNED FOR POWER.

NON-RENEWABLE RESOURCE: A NATURAL RESOURCE THAT CANNOT BE REMADE OR REPLENISHED.

EGYPTIAN SCIENTISTS AND BUILDERS USED ADVANCED TECHNOLOGY TO BUILD THEIR TOMBS AND TEMPLES, MANY OF WHICH HAVE SURVIVED THE PASSAGE OF THOUSANDS OF YEARS.

FOSSIL FUELS

Oil, coal, and natural gas are examples of **fossil fuels**. Fossil fuels are formed from the remains of dead plants and animals deep in the earth's crust. After millions of years, they turn into oil or natural gas. Fossil fuels have been responsible for advancing industrial development around the world. However, burning fossil fuels adds toxic chemicals to the environment and contributes to the problem of global **climate change**. They are also **non-renewable resources**, meaning they will eventually run out.

THE COUNTRIES OF NORTH AFRICA

Morocco, Algeria, Tunisia, Libya, and Egypt make up the region of North Africa. Ancient Greeks used the name Libya, taken from the name of a coastal tribe, to describe land south of the Sahara. In 146 BC, the Romans named their first province "Africa" in what is modern-day Tunisia.

Morocco, Tunisia, and Algeria are home to the Atlas Mountains, which are part of an immense mountain range. The mountains run along much of the Mediterranean coast, making the area difficult to live in, except for the valleys. Much of the rest of North Africa is in the Sahara. These natural barriers create challenges for the advancement of trade and technology in the region. However, they have also historically provided protection from invading nations for the area's small, scattered tribes.

FAST FACT

NORTH AFRICA WAS ONE OF THE ANCIENT WORLD'S RICHEST REGIONS. TRADERS THERE MADE FORTUNES SELLING GEMSTONES, GOLD, AND OTHER VALUABLE METALS.

TRADITIONAL ECONOMY: AN ECONOMY BASED ON SUBSISTENCE FARMING OR CUSTOMARY ACTIVITIES.

THE LAND WHERE THE SUN SETS

The North African countries bordering the Mediterranean Sea are called the Maghreb, which means "West." While much of the south of the Maghreb is in the desert, there are northern sections in the Atlas Mountains where it rains over 4 inches (10.2 cm) per year. With the unforgiving desert on one side and steep mountain ranges on the other, the first settlers of the Maghreb were a close-knit culture. They developed local trading systems that drove their **traditional economy** for centuries.

BEFORE MODERN TECHNOLOGY, THE MEDITERRANEAN'S JAGGED COAST—WITH FEW NATURAL HARBORS—MADE INTERNATIONAL TRADE DIFFICULT.

SOUTHWEST ASIA

Southwest Asia is made up of Turkey, Iran, Iraq, Syria, Lebanon, Israel, Jordan, Saudi Arabia, and the rest of the Arabian Peninsula (including Qatar and Kuwait). Many people also refer to this region as the Middle East.

More than 278 million people live in southwest Asia, more than half in Turkey and Iran. Much of the region is uninhabited, with a dry desert climate and little rain or fresh vegetation. Because of the harsh climate, the area had little economic growth until the discovery of oil in the 20th century. The wealth generated from the **export** of oil changed the region forever. It also made southwest Asia the center of several world crises, because of other countries' attempts to control the oil-rich land, or due to cultural conflicts between the local people.

FAST FACT

NOT EVERY COUNTRY IN SOUTHWEST ASIA BENEFITS FROM OIL PRODUCTION. IN TURKEY, MANUFACTURING INDUSTRIES LIKE FOOD, BEVERAGES, CHEMICALS, AND CLOTHING MAKE UP ONE-THIRD OF THE **GROSS DOMESTIC PRODUCT (GDP)** AND EMPLOY ALMOST 25 PERCENT OF THE WORKFORCE.

GROSS DOMESTIC PRODUCT (GDP): THE TOTAL VALUE OF GOODS PRODUCED AND SERVICES PROVIDED IN A COUNTRY DURING ONE YEAR.

TO FARM SUCCESSFULLY IN A DESERT CLIMATE, PEOPLE IN SOUTHWEST ASIA HAVE BEEN USING IRRIGATION SYSTEMS LIKE THIS FOR CENTURIES.

AN EXTREME CONTINENT

Covering 17 million square miles (44 million sq km), Asia is the largest of all the continents and takes up almost one-third of Earth's surface. Four billion people—or more than 60 percent of the world's population—call the continent home. Asia also has the most extreme weather of all the continents, from the **tundra** in the far north to the tropical temperatures and heavy rainfall in the south. In southwest Asia, where the land has been dry since ancient times, countries have adapted by developing irrigation technology to keep farms usable.

THE BEGINNING OF CIVILIZATION

The earliest human civilizations developed in the Fertile Crescent from around 5000 to 3000 BC. The fertile, or rich, area of the Tigris and Euphrates Rivers is in what is now Iraq. The rivers made the valley good for growing crops, inspiring the Greeks to name it Mesopotamia, or "land between the rivers."

Ancient peoples worked together to farm and build irrigation systems. For the first time, people consistently had enough to eat without having to move from place to place. Civilization was born.

These early peoples created city-states, small communities that governed themselves. Many inventions and ideas came from these societies. The wheel first appeared around 3500 BC, and some of the world's oldest boats were found in the region. The earliest examples of math also came from Mesopotamian states, dating back to 3000 BC.

BIRTHPLACE OF RELIGION

Christianity, Judaism, and Islam all originated in ancient southwest Asia. The three major religions are similar in their practice of **monotheism**. Religion has played a major role in politics and government in the region for centuries. Iran, for example, backs up its laws with religious beliefs. In recent decades, strict religious control has made some regional governments less stable. This instability keeps foreign investors away and slows local economic growth and development.

MONOTHEISM: BELIEF IN ONE GOD.

THE EARLY PEOPLE OF MESOPOTAMIA DEVELOPED A TYPE OF WRITING CALLED CUNEIFORM, MADE UP OF SYMBOLS CARVED INTO CLAY TABLETS OR STONES.

FAST FACT

THE KINGDOM OF BABYLON BROUGHT A SYSTEM OF BANKING TO MESOPOTAMIA, INCLUDING MAXIMUM (NOT MINIMUM) WAGES ASSIGNED BY LAW. THE KINGDOM OF ASSYRIA, LOCATED JUST NORTH OF BABYLON, WAS THE FIRST TO MAKE ITS WEAPONS OUT OF IRON, GIVING IT A POWERFUL MILITARY ADVANTAGE.

CARTHAGE AND ROMAN AFRICA

North Africa was settled in 1000 BC by the **Phoenicians**. Carthage was the largest Phoenician colony and an **imperial** power. The government established settlements on the coast to control the trading industry, and Carthage soon became the richest city in the world. Carthaginians manufactured and traded fabrics, food, and raw metals for gold, silver, and tin.

Rome destroyed Carthage and took over North Africa in 146 BC. Small cities were established with local leaders—typically wealthy landowners—and the residents were tenant farmers. By the first century AD, African grain exports supplied two-thirds of the demand of the city of Rome. Technology was used to expand existing ports and build sophisticated road systems. Roman control of North Africa ended in the fifth century AD.

THE BLADE INDUSTRY

Tens of thousands of years ago, flake tools were used for hunting in North Africa. These tools were shaped by flaking small pieces off a larger stone to make a sharp tool. The earliest traces of flake tools have been found in Algeria, Morocco, and Tunisia. These peoples used stone because they did not have access or the ability to work metal. Similar flake tools have also been found along the coast of Libya dating between 15,000 and 10,000 BC, making blade manufacturing one of the earliest known industries

FAST FACT

IN THE EARLY SEVENTH CENTURY, ARABIC MUSLIMS INVADED NORTH AFRICA. MOST OF NORTH AFRICA FELL UNDER MUSLIM RULE, AND THE AREA IS PREDOMINANTLY MUSLIM TODAY.

PHOENICIANS: INHABITANTS OF ANCIENT SOUTHWEST ASIA WHERE LEBANON, PARTS OF SYRIA, AND ISRAEL NOW ARE LOCATED.

THESE RUINS DATE BACK TO ANCIENT CARTHAGE, ONE OF NORTH AFRICA'S MOST POWERFUL HISTORICAL CIVILIZATIONS.

ISLAMIC CONQUEST AND COLLAPSE

By AD 670, Islamic culture had spread throughout southwest Asia. The last great Islamic empire was the Ottoman (Turkish) Empire, which ruled from 1453 until World War I in the early 20th century. During the war, the Ottomans allied with Germany. Europe responded by attacking Mesopotamia, Libya, and Egypt, and the Ottoman Empire fell apart.

Following the Ottoman collapse, European powers began occupying southwest Asia. Britain and France divided up the land based on their interests. New borders were drawn with no regard for the **cultural landscape** of the region. The British had encouraged an uprising of Arab **nationalists** against the Ottoman government during the war, promising them independence. After the war ended, they broke their promises and imposed imperial rule. These factors caused political and economic instability in the region that continues today.

FAST FACT

T. E. LAWRENCE "OF ARABIA" WAS A BRITISH SOLDIER WHO SUPPORTED THE ARABIAN REBELLION AGAINST THE OTTOMAN EMPIRE DURING WORLD WAR I. HIS ATTACKS DISRUPTED THE DELIVERY OF SUPPLIES AND DISTRACTED THE TURKS.

CULTURAL LANDSCAPE: A GEOGRAPHIC AREA, INCLUDING CULTURAL AND NATURAL RESOURCES ASSOCIATED WITH A HISTORIC EVENT, ACTIVITY, OR PERSON OR EXHIBITING OTHER CULTURAL VALUES.

IMPORTED: BROUGHT INTO A COUNTRY FROM SOMEWHERE ELSE.

FAILED FOREIGN POLICY

Hundreds of thousands of Arabs were killed during World War I, and more died of starvation from lack of **imported** food. The French and British wanted to rebuild the agricultural economy, but often made decisions based on their political interests and the interests of their wealthy investors. This increased Arab resentment toward European leadership and helped inspire a nationalist movement that would eventually result in the independence of southwestern Asian nations from European rule.

T. E. LAWRENCE SUPPORTED ARABIAN INTERESTS, BUT EUROPEAN POWERS TOOK ADVANTAGE OF THE REGION'S NEW INDEPENDENCE TO MAKE THEMSELVES RICHER.

COLONIZATION IN NORTH AFRICA

European **colonization** in North Africa resulted in political conflict, which in turn hurt the economy. When the French took over Algeria in 1830, its victory came with a price paid by the local Muslim community. Their political rights were denied. Immigration from Europe dramatically increased the Algerian population, but the country's wealth was drained away to European countries. Large amounts of wheat and wine were produced and exported to France while the locals lived in poverty.

As in southwest Asia, the people of North Africa eventually became upset at the growing wealth of the European countries while they continued to suffer. Rebellions broke out in Libya and Algeria, and the French gave independence to Tunisia and Morocco in an effort to end the violence. War and distrust made it impossible for the economy to develop.

FAST FACT

AN ARAB-ISRAELI CONFLICT BEGAN IN 1948 WHEN ARAB COUNTRIES UNITED TO OPPOSE THE STATE OF ISRAEL. THIS ONGOING CONFLICT HAS AFFECTED THE ENTIRE REGION'S ECONOMY, AS OTHER WORLD POWERS HAVE ARGUED OVER WHICH SIDE TO SUPPORT.

FUNDAMENTALISM: A MOVEMENT STRESSING STRICT AND LITERAL ADHERENCE TO A SET OF PRINCIPLES.

THE EFFECTS OF WORLD WAR II ON SOUTHWEST ASIA

After World War II, southwest Asia was no longer under European control, but the long-term economic effects would be devastating. As a rejection of European leadership, many locals looked to Islamic **fundamentalism** as the answer to their problems. This approach to government has caused conflict with many Western nations, including the United States, and scared off foreign investors. This has slowed economic growth—aside from the sale of oil. In the 21st century, the economies of some southwest Asian countries, including Iran and Iraq, are still struggling to develop.

MIDDLE EASTERN TIMELINE

3500 BC
Evidence of the first wheel appears in modern-day Iraq

AD 642
Arabs conquer Egypt and spread Islam to North Africa

1517–1918
The Ottoman Empire rules much of southwest Asia and North Africa

1908
William D'Arcy discovers oil in modern-day Iran

1918
Britain and France take over areas of Middle East following World War I

1935
The ancient area known as Persia officially becomes the country of Iran

1945
The Arab League is founded following World War II

1946
Jordan gains independence from Britain; Syria gains independence from France

1959
Companies discover oil in Libya

1979–1991
Conflict spreads across the Middle East, including the Iran-Iraq War and the Gulf War; economic growth slows because of political instability

2010
Economic instability in the Middle East continues as pro-democracy protestors in the region seek to overthrow their governments during the Arab Spring

2017–2019
Iranian protestors take to the streets, unhappy with the country's struggling economy

BLACK GOLD

Few things have had a greater impact on southwest Asia or North Africa than the discovery of oil. Historically, southwest Asia was made up mostly of **nomadic** people who carried their tents and belongings with them in search of places with green grass and clean water. The hot, dry climate made farmable land scarce. Most food had to be imported, and the average person was very poor.

Oil was discovered in Persia (now Iran) by William D'Arcy in 1908, who founded the Anglo-Persian Oil Company. Britain became the Anglo-Persian Company's biggest investor during World War I and was able to **modernize** its military using the natural resource. As the automobile industry grew, so did the demand for gas. The Anglo-Persian Oil Company later became the multinational oil company British **Petroleum** (BP).

MODERNIZE: TO MAKE MORE ADVANCED OR MODERN.

FAST FACT

DURING THE EARLY 1980s, LIBYAN LEADER MUAMMAR AL-QADDAFI SPENT BILLIONS OF DOLLARS ON MILITARY PROGRAMS IN OPPOSITION OF U.S. SUPPORT OF ISRAEL. THE UNITED STATES RESPONDED WITH **SANCTIONS**, WHICH IMPACTED LIBYA'S OIL PRODUCTION AND HURT ITS ECONOMY.

WILLIAM D'ARCY WAS JUST ABOUT TO GIVE UP HIS SEVEN-YEAR SEARCH WHEN HE STRUCK OIL ON A PATCH OF PERSIAN DESERT AND CHANGED THE WORLD ECONOMY FOREVER.

SOCIALISM: ANY OF VARIOUS ECONOMIC AND POLITICAL THEORIES ADVOCATING COLLECTIVE OR GOVERNMENTAL OWNERSHIP AND ADMINISTRATION OF THE MEANS OF PRODUCTION AND DISTRIBUTION OF GOODS.

INSTANT WEALTH

Libya was one of the poorest countries in the world until oil was discovered in 1959. At the time, the country was ruled by King Idris, who profited from the oil sales while the people remained poor. In 1969, colonel Muammar al-Qaddafi led a revolt that resulted in the overthrow of the king. Al-Qaddafi became head of state and instituted a system of government based on **socialism**. Oil profits were now used to support technological development, construction projects, a modern education system, and the military.

Oil was discovered in Saudi Arabia in 1938. Before then, the Saudi economy was supported by tourism from Muslims traveling to the religion's holy land. Now, oil sales make up 92 percent of Saudi Arabia's budget. Southwest Asia has more than two-thirds of the world's oil reserves, and the Arabian peninsula (Saudi Arabia, Iran, Iraq, Kuwait, and the United Arab Emirates) contains more than 90 percent of those reserves and at least 60 percent of the world's supply.

U.S. dependence on petroleum has opened doors to political relationships with the Saudis. However, it has also been a source of criticism. Some believe that Saudi Arabia's alliance with the United States gives them an unfair role in U.S. policy decisions that affect the entire region.

OPEC

The oil industry was once controlled by large U.S. and European companies. The actual resource was located in poor countries with limited technology, which depended on the foreign companies to remove, refine, and sell the oil. These businesses kept prices low and took most of the profit. Five countries—Iran, Iraq, Kuwait, Saudi Arabia, and Venezuela—founded the Organization of the Petroleum Exporting Countries (**OPEC**) in 1960. OPEC member nations control about two-thirds of the world's petroleum reserves and make policies on oil prices and production.

OPEC: A MULTINATIONAL GROUP FORMED TO COORDINATE WORLDWIDE PETROLEUM POLICY AND PRICES.

LIBYA WAS ONE OF THE MEMBERS OF OPEC THAT EMBARGOED THE SALE OF OIL TO THE UNITED STATES DURING THE ARAB-ISRAELI WAR.

EMBARGO: A GOVERNMENT ORDER THAT RESTRICTS TRADE.

FAST FACT

IN THE 1970s, THE ARAB MEMBERS OF OPEC PLACED AN **EMBARGO** ON THE UNITED STATES, RESULTING IN GAS SHORTAGES AND SKY-HIGH PRICES IN THE WESTERN WORLD.

THE RICH GET RICHER

After the rise of OPEC, the Arabian Peninsula suddenly had a strong economy. People immigrated to the area, which created a healthy labor force. They gained access to new technology, education, and research. These developments attracted foreign investors to the region—but not everyone benefited equally.

Saudi Arabia has one of the most productive economies in the world, but many residents remain poor. This is partially because the oil industry employs millions of foreign workers, leaving little opportunity for Saudis.

Saudi Arabian policies are based on Islamic law, and certain types of business and industry are forbidden. Women have historically not been allowed to join the workforce, limiting the number of available native workers. Saudi Arabia has started investing in new industries, including agriculture and the service industry, in hopes of creating new jobs.

FAST FACT

MANY OIL-RICH NATIONS ARE RULED BY **MONARCHS** WHO DON'T SHARE THE NATION'S WEALTH. ADDITIONALLY, CENTURIES-OLD POLITICAL AND RELIGIOUS CONFLICTS PUT A STRAIN ON THE LOCAL ECONOMY.

THE JEBEL POWER STATION IN DUBAI IS THE LARGEST POWER AND WATER **DESALINIZATION** PLANT IN THE UNITED ARAB EMIRATES.

DESALINIZATION: THE PROCESS OF REMOVING SALT FROM SEAWATER TO MAKE FRESH WATER.

SCARCITY: A CONDITION WHERE THERE IS NOT ENOUGH OF A PRODUCT TO MEET DEMAND FOR THE PRODUCT.

DESALINIZATION

Water is important in many parts of a successful society. Because of its water **scarcity**, Saudi Arabia has long had to come up with creative ways to keep people and farms supplied with the resource. Today, the country leads the world in water desalinization (also known as desalination). This is a process that turns seawater into drinking water. About 50 percent of the country's drinking water comes from desalinization. Saudi Arabia is home to 31 desalinization plants operated by more than 10,000 employees.

NATIONS WITHOUT OIL

Economies of non–oil producing countries in southwest Asia and North Africa are much different. Egypt produces some oil, but its main exports are cotton, rice, and citrus fruit. Its growing manufacturing industry produces chemicals, clothing, and cement. Egypt struggled to recover from its 2011 revolution, in which its monarchy was overthrown. Other nations in the region, including Tunisia and Libya, also had revolutions in 2011 as part of the Arab Spring.

Egypt's revolution hurt the economy by scaring away tourists and foreign investors. The price of food, fuel, and rent skyrocketed while salaries stayed the same. A lack of **infrastructure** and technology has made rebuilding difficult. The number of Egyptians living in poverty has doubled over the past 20 years. However, the economy started to improve in 2018 after policy reforms.

FAST FACT

EGYPT GENERATES **REVENUE** FROM ITS CONTROL OF THE SUEZ CANAL, A **TRANSPORTATION CORRIDOR** ACROSS A NARROW PIECE OF LAND IN EGYPT. IT'S THE SHORTEST WATER ROUTE BETWEEN EUROPE AND EASTERN ASIA AND ONE OF THE BUSIEST SHIPPING LANES IN THE WORLD.

TRANSPORTATION CORRIDOR: AN AREA OF LAND THAT INCLUDES LINES OF TRANSPORTATION, LIKE RAILROADS, HIGHWAYS, AND CANALS.

THE SUEZ CANAL CELEBRATED ITS 150TH BIRTHDAY ON NOVEMBER 17, 2019.

THE COUNTRY IN THE MIDDLE

Jordan's location in the middle of Syria, Iraq, Saudi Arabia, and Israel has great importance. It supports the United States in an effort to establish peace in the region. Without reserves of natural resources like oil, Jordan's economy relies on countries like the United States for financial assistance. Jordan has been the center of several refugee crises in Israel and Syria, increasing the population and making it difficult to import enough food, clothing, and shelter. Currently, 14 percent of its population is poor.

ECONOMIC GROWTH AND OBSTACLES

The industrialized world has an ever-increasing demand for energy. In 2018, oil exporters in southwest Asia and North Africa had an average economic growth of almost 2 percent. Economic reforms in Egypt and the discovery of natural gas reserves caused its economy to grow even faster. Non–oil producing countries Morocco and Tunisia saw their economies grow from increases in agriculture and tourism.

Other countries in the region remain affected by conflict. Libya's oil production has been much lower since its civil war in 2011, when production was totally disrupted. Sanctions imposed by the United States against Iran have caused a severe drop in the country's oil exports. The war in Syria has raised unemployment to above 50 percent and it will cost more than $200 billion to repair the country's infrastructure.

RECESSION: A PERIOD OF REDUCED ECONOMIC ACTIVITY.

FAST FACT

DESPITE AN ECONOMIC **RECESSION** IN THE LATE 2010s, TURKEY HAS BEEN ABLE TO KEEP UNEMPLOYMENT LOW AND MAINTAIN A SOLID UPPER MIDDLE CLASS. IT HAS A LARGE MANUFACTURING INDUSTRY AND IS ONE OF THE LEADING PRODUCERS OF STEEL IN SOUTHWEST ASIA.

FUTURE CHALLENGES

The main challenge facing the nations of North Africa and southwest Asia is the lack of long-term conflict resolution. Decades-old tensions have resulted in costly wars and massive loss of life. Until these tensions are settled, uncertainty and security concerns will keep business out of the region. Government reform must also be addressed. Many North African and southwest Asian nations are governed by corrupt leaders who rule out of self-interest.

OIL SUPPORTS THE ECONOMIES OF MANY SOUTHWEST ASIAN AND NORTH AFRICAN COUNTRIES. HOWEVER, RELYING SO MUCH ON A SINGLE PRODUCT CAN BE RISKY—IF PRICES FALL, THE ECONOMY WILL SUFFER.

COUNTRIES THAT ARE MOST DEPENDENT ON OIL TO FUEL ECONOMY GROWTH

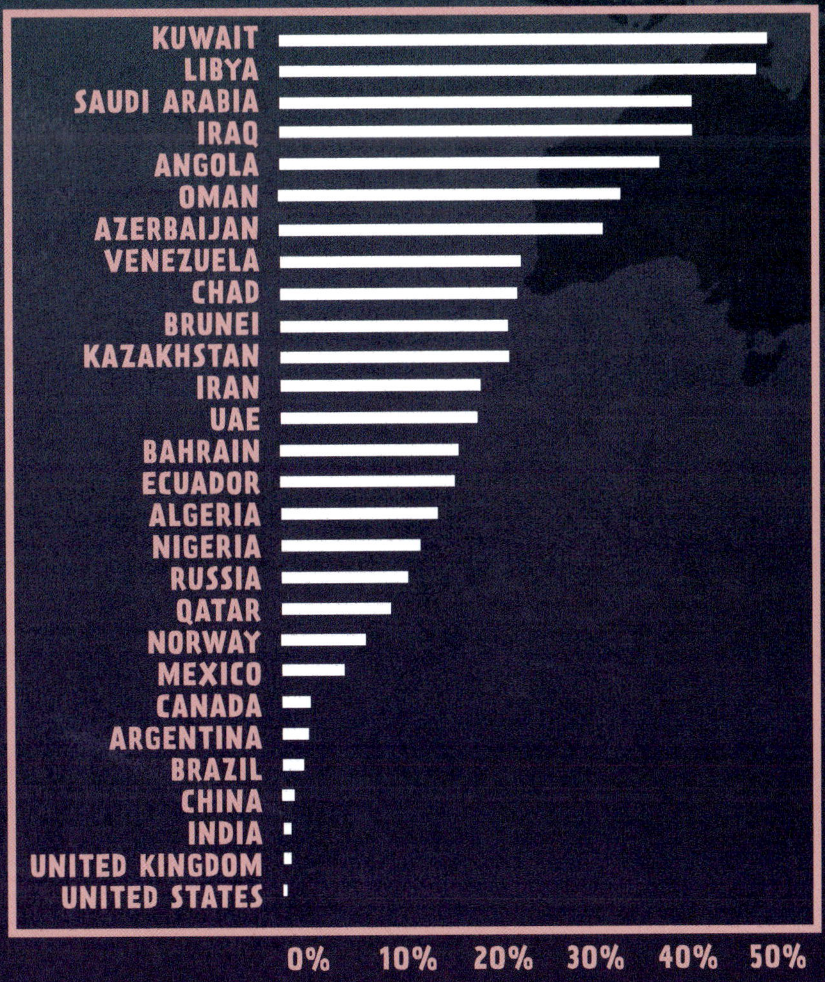

A BRIDGE BETWEEN TRADITION AND TECHNOLOGY

While industrial powers such as the United States continue to grow, the nations that provide them energy often fall behind. However, as countries in southwest Asia and North Africa start using science and technology to harness **renewable resources**, they are catching up. North Africa has an abundance of solar and wind energy resources. Between 2010 and 2015, North African countries increased wind and solar production by two to three times.

The nations of southwest Asia and North Africa have often been deeply divided. In modern times, traditions are competing with new technology. Young people want free trade while the old laws keep economies controlled. Finding ways to bridge the gap and move the region into the future—while respecting its sacred history—is the key to the area's economic success.

FAST FACT

THE GLOBAL COVID-19 VIRUS PANDEMIC, OR WIDESPREAD ILLNESS, THAT BEGAN IN 2019 WILL HAVE A LASTING EFFECT ON ECONOMIES IN THIS REGION AND AROUND THE WORLD.

MANY NATIONS OF NORTH AFRICA AND SOUTHWEST ASIA HAVE STARTED DOING THEIR PART TO KEEP THE AIR CLEAN AND THE LANDSCAPE BEAUTIFUL.

RENEWABLE RESOURCE: A NATURAL RESOURCE THAT CAN BE REPLENISHED NATURALLY.

THE SAKAKA SOLAR PLANT

The Sakaka project is Saudi Arabia's first large solar farm, developed as part of its national initiatives to advance clean energy. It's estimated that the farm will generate enough solar power for 45,000 households, eliminating approximately 474,000 tons (430,000 metric tons) of toxins from the environment per year. The project also has a 100 percent local employment rate, with 90 percent of the workers made up of young people in the area, boosting the local economy. The Sakaka solar plant opened in November 2019.

GLOSSARY

climate change: Long-term change in Earth's climate, caused primarily by human activities such as burning oil and natural gas.

colonization: The act of making or establishing a settlement in a new territory that maintains ties to a distant parent state.

export: To sell a product outside of its country of origin.

imperial: Related to an empire.

infrastructure: The equipment and structures needed for a country, state, or region to function properly.

irrigation: The watering of a dry area by man-made means in order to grow plants.

monarch: The head of a monarchy, such as a king or queen.

nationalist: One who supports national independence.

nomadic: Having to do with people who move from place to place.

petroleum: An oily natural resource that is the source of fuel, such as gasoline.

revenue: Money that is generated by selling something.

sanction: A governmental policy that aims to force another nation to stop an action or agree to other terms.

tundra: Geographical area that is typically cold and without forests.

FOR MORE INFORMATION

BOOKS

Atinuke. *Africa, Amazing Africa*. London, U.K.: Walker Books, 2020.

McKenna, Amy. *The History of Northern Africa*. New York, NY: Rosen Publishing, 2011.

Tyler, Madeline. *Cultural Contributions from the Middle East: Hospitals, Algebra, and More*. New York, NY: PowerKids Press, 2019.

WEBSITES

Africa Facts
www.kids-world-travel-guide.com/africa-facts.html
This website offers a list of unusual and interesting facts about Africa.

Ancient Africa: Ancient Carthage
www.ducksters.com/history/africa/ancient_carthage.php
On this site, users can learn more about Carthage, the ancient North African city.

The Middle East
easyscienceforkids.com/all-about-the-middle-east
This website gives readers the chance to discover more about the complicated history of the Middle East.

Publisher's note to educators and parents: Our editors have carefully reviewed these websites to ensure that they are suitable for students. Many websites change frequently, however, and we cannot guarantee that a site's future contents will continue to meet our high standards of quality and educational value. Be advised that students should be closely supervised whenever they access the internet.

INDEX